50 Shades of Light

By

Jody Burks and Susan Neese

To Rose
To God be the glory!
Susan *and Jody*

CROSSLINK
PUBLISHING

50 Shades of Light

CrossLink Publishing
www.crosslinkpublishing.com

ISBN 978-1-936746-39-2

This book is dedicated to:

Casey, Mandy, Michelle, and Tif

Preface

In the midst of the darkness in our world we are so certain of, and so thankful for, God's brilliant light.

We lift up our Lord and Savior and thank Him for lighting our path. We pray that these Scriptures and thoughts bring comfort to you and a desire to pick up the torch and carry God's light into the world.

May God richly bless you,

~ Jody and Susan

And God said, "Let there be light, and there was light."
Genesis 1:3 (NASB)

The very first command of God in the word of God is "Let there be light." (Gen. 1:3) And after He saw that it was good, the next thing He did was to separate it from the darkness. The fact that He saw that it was good and separated it from the darkness somehow indicates the darkness was not desirable. Things can go unnoticed in the dark. The dark can hide secrets. It is interesting that light can dispel darkness, but not the other way around.

Some things never change; it is still God's desire that the light be separated from the darkness. We, as Christians, are to walk in the light as He is in the light. We are to be juxtaposed to the dark in order to show the radiance of God. As His light shines in us we, too, should expel the darkness.

juxtaposed   placed side by side   adjacent
close proximity
so as to permit comparison and contrast

There is no prettier or healthier place to be than walking in the light of the Lord. His word promises us that He will walk with us and whisper in our ear which way to go. He has an eternal path for us on which to walk that leads to the light found in His glory.

We might say, "how can we spread the gospel if we separate ourselves from the darkness?" There is a huge difference between walking in the dark and ministering to the dark. God expects us to reach out to the lost, to help the lost, to pray for the lost, but not to become one of the lost in order to spread the gospel. The best way to minister to others is by letting God's glorious light shine through us in our everyday lives. Just as the light draws the moth, God's light in us will draw the hardest of hearts to Him.

And God said, "Let there be light, and there was light." Genesis 1:3 (NASB)

As we pray how others might see us, let us agree with God and say, "Let there be light."

_____

_____

_____

_____

_____

_____

_____

_____

_____

_____

_____

_____

_____

_____

And the Lord was going before them in a pillar of cloud by day to lead them on the way, and in a pillar of fire by night to give them light, that they might travel by day and by night.
Exodus 13:21 (NASB)

The opening lines of a famous hymn go like this: "All the way my Savior leads me; What have I to ask beside? Can I doubt His tender mercy, Who thro' life has been my guide?" These lines were penned by Fanny Crosby, a woman known to have written thousands of hymns. Many of those hymns speak of God's loving guidance in her life, with her faith showing through them, one after another.

When Fanny was just a few weeks old, she was stricken with an eye infection. Never fully recovering from it, she went through life blind. She could only discern the dark from the light. When we reflect on some of her hymns like "Blessed Assurance," "Rescue the Perishing," and "Safe in the Arms of Jesus," we can see that hers was no little faith. When asked by others about her blindness, she considered it a true blessing from God. Isn't it interesting that perhaps her vision was clearer than many of ours?

I have been thinking that we would be better off if we could clearly discern the dark from the light. Maybe that is all we really need to get along in this life. I know I have always struggled with poor eyesight, yearning to see more clearly. Having gone through several pairs of glasses and Lasik eye surgery, I still find that I don't always see matters very clearly.

I recently spent hours pouring over some of Fanny Crosby's beautiful hymns and have decided her physical blindness made her spiritual vision all the more acute. Oh to see the things of God so clearly. Rather
than focusing on the clarity of the situation, perhaps it would behoove *BE SUITABLE FOR* us to just discern the dark from the light. If we follow the One who called Himself the Light of the World, we will never be led astray.

5

And the Lord was going before them in a pillar of cloud by day to lead them
on the way, and in a pillar of fire by night to give them light, that they might
travel by day and by night.
Exodus 13:21 (NASB)

Light of the World, as Fanny asked in her hymn – "How can I doubt Your
tender mercy, when through life You have been my guide?" What a
mercy it is to know that You still lead us by Your light day and night.
Lord, I pray that you would help me see the things that have eternal value
more clearly. May I follow the Light all the days of my life. Amen.

For You are my lamp, O Lord,
and my God lightens my darkness.
II Samuel 22:29 (ESV)

II Samuel, chapter two, is set out in my Bible as "David's Song of Deliverance". Some commentaries read that this heading refers to David's deliverance from all of his enemies, and we know that David had numerous trials and enemies. In this particular instance, God has rescued David from the hands of Saul and David sang out to the Lord with an emotional outburst of love and thanksgiving.

David calls the Lord his rock and fortress. What a powerful image this gives me. I see David tucked behind the huge protective barrier as the tumultuous waves crash against the wall. Can you see God's hand shielding his beloved? Can you see yourself behind that rock with David?

David says that in his distress he shouts out for the Lord and the Lord heard his cry and the "earth reeled and rocked" (vs8) as the Lord came from the heaven to rescue David from his enemy. God wants to be our protector. He wants us to call out to Him when we are put to the test and He will boldly answer our plea if we are in the right place with Him. David tells us that "...He rescued me because He delighted in me" (vs20). God is delighted in us when we have a relationship with Him. He cannot be delighted if He does not know us, and He cannot know us if we do not ever go to Him in prayer and praise.

When God knows us, we can be assured of protection. David reminds us that God lightens our darkness and that "His way is perfect" (vs31)! In this dark world, I do not want to pass up the security of being shielded by our Lord. I desire to know Him in ways so intimate that He will be delighted in me and run to rescue me in my times of need. Friend, I want that for you too.

For You are my lamp, O Lord,
and my God lightens my darkness.
2 Samuel 22:29 (ESV)

Dearest Loving Protector,

You are such an amazing God and I don't deserve Your diligent vigil over me. Show me how to draw nearer to You so that I might live in ways that delight and honor You. Thank You, God, for desiring to protect and shield me. Thank You for reminding me that Your way is perfect.

_____

_____

_____

_____

_____

_____

_____

_____

_____

_____

_____

By a pillar of cloud you lead them in the day, and by a pillar of fire
in the night to light for them the way in which they should go.
Nehemiah 9:19 (NKJV)

N ehemiah was an amazing man. As the cupbearer to King Artaxerxes, Nehemiah had a comfortable life and a highly respected position. However, when he learned that the walls of Jerusalem had been broken down and destroyed by fire, Nehemiah mourned. After a time of fasting and praying to God, Nehemiah knew that he must go and rebuild the wall. He then approached his king, received permission to leave, and went about doing God's business.

Midway through his endeavor, Nehemiah met with resistance and obstacles. He became very discouraged, but in the midst of his darkness, Nehemiah turned to God. His prayer of praise, confession, and petition first set out the Lord as the Most High by naming the magnificent things the Lord had done for his creation. Nehemiah followed this with a reminder to God that He saw the afflictions of the followers in Egypt and led them from their bondage; even parting the Red Sea to allow their full escape. Finally, Nehemiah asked the Lord to be his light and lead the rebuilding of the wall of Jerusalem. That wall was built, in spite of the opposition, in fifty-one days. God had a plan and used Nehemiah to work that plan, but only because Nehemiah followed the Light of the Lord.

How many times have you been struggling midway into a project then realized that it should not have been so difficult? Maybe it is because you left God out of the equation. When we turn to God, ask him to lead us, then follow the light that he holds to shine our way, we will succeed. God will bless our efforts when we are within His plan; when we are following His path. Remember the Red Sea?

By a pillar of cloud you lead them in the day, and by a pillar of fire
in the night to light for them the way in which they should go.
Nehemiah 9:19 (NKJV)

Thank You, Father God, for loving me as much as You loved our fathers who fled from Egypt. Thank You for reminding me that You are holding the light, illuminating the path that You wish for me to travel. Lord, keep me on that path and following Your light.

_____

_____

_____

_____

_____

_____

_____

_____

_____

_____

_____

_____

He has redeemed my soul from going down into the pit,
and my life shall look upon the light.
Job 33:28 (ESV)

Oh what a vision of love Jesus has given us. He willingly came to this dirty, sinful, world to die on the cross so that we might not perish. Jesus took on all of my sins and all of your sins so that we might have the promise of eternal life, basking in the light of our Father in heaven.

Why then, do we so often willingly step into the darkness? Jesus must be devastated every time we make that choice to turn our back on the lighted path. I can see the tears on His cheek as He gazes down on all these souls. Souls that He loved enough to give the light of eternity, only to have us cover it up so we might hide from its brightness. Souls that choose contemporary culture over our Lord and Savior, even when He promises us eternal Light. Oh how our Jesus must weep!

Turn to the Light. Jesus gives us that Light and wishes nothing more than for us to step away from the pit. Let's make Jesus' loving sacrifice be fruitful. Can you see his beautiful smile when He hears the voice of his child say "Yes Jesus. Light my path so that I may not be a victim of the pit"?

He has redeemed my soul from going down into
the pit, and my life shall look upon the light.
Job 33:28 (ESV)

Dear loving Jesus,

Thank You for your gift of Light. Keep it shining on me in ways that make me desire to make You smile. Thank You for restoring me so that I might have eternal life in Your glorious heavenly light.

_____

_____

_____

_____

_____

_____

_____

_____

_____

_____

_____

_____

_____

There are many who say, "Who will show us some good? Lift up
the light of your face upon us, O Lord!"
Psalm 4:6 (ESV)

As a child I was not so very adept at praying to God. I had two standard prayers I used: the One many of us know as "Now I lay me down to sleep," and my mealtime prayer – "God is good. God is great, and we thank Him for this food. Amen." Little did I know what a profound truth is found in this child's prayer. God is indeed good.

The Scriptures tell us that every good thing comes from God. Don't you love it when the Word of God uses words like "all" or "every"? It leaves no room for debate. I believe because the Scriptures say "God is love," everything He does is motivated by His love for us. This certainly lines up with the concept of all good things come from God.

Looking at the question posed in the above verse found in Psalms –
Who will show us good? It only makes sense that the One who loves
us most would be the One who shows us some good. The amazing
truth in this verse, however, is that the Lord needs only to lift up His
countenance and let His radiance shine upon us to exude goodness.

As we go through life wanting "good things" we need to realize the
source of all good things is God, Himself. While there are those
stumbling about in the dark it seems they must have their backs to the
Lord, for it only requires looking into His face to find His favor. Let's
turn toward God and accept the goodness He has for us.

There are many who say," Who will show us some good? Lift up
the light of your face upon us, O Lord!"
Psalm 4:6 (ESV)

Gracious God, full of goodness, we long to see Your face. We confess
we too often are looking away from You rather than allowing the
radiance of Your face to shine upon us. Turn us around, Lord, so we
might look full into Your wonderful face. Amen.

_____

_____

_____

_____

_____

_____

_____

_____

_____

_____

_____

_____

The Lord is my light and my salvation; Whom shall I fear? The Lord is
the defense of my life; Whom shall I dread?
Psalm 27:1 (NASB)

This verse's wording suggests that because the Lord is my light and my salvation, I have nothing to fear. The fact that the Lord is my salvation covers my eternity; death is not something to dread. It is the first part of the verse that can be harder to comprehend.

The longer we have been in the Christian community, the more we hear certain phrases batted around like - get into the word, praise the Lord, and this one under scrutiny: the Lord is my light. What exactly does it mean when we say the Lord is my light? The word of God repeatedly tells us that we were once in darkness and after accepting Jesus as our Savior, we are in the light. Because God is light and we have His Holy Spirit within us, we have this internal light that can radiate out of us for several purposes.

As we allow the Lord to be our light we can see where we are going in this world of darkness. Because the Christian life is not always mountain top experiences we need the light of the Lord as we trek through the valley of the shadow of death. Though we know death is not to be feared the journey in the shadows can be, but His light shows us the way.

His light also can affect others with whom we come in contact. Often times we "see" things more clearly than others, especially those who don't know the Lord. Once they see the truth that accompanies the light, they may want what we have – Jesus. This is one reason the word exhorts us not to hide our light under a basket, there is a hungry world out there longing for a light, oftentimes a light of hope. Hope generally replaces fear when it is genuine. As I allow the Lord's light to shine through me, I bring hope to a dark and weary world.

The Lord is my light and my salvation; Whom shall I fear? The Lord is
the defense of my life; Whom shall I dread?
Psalm 27:1 (NASB)

Lord, You are my Light, and I have nothing to fear. I pray that I might
be seen as a light in my little corner of the world. I pray that Your
Light will not only show me the way, but also show others. Amen.

_____

_____

_____

_____

_____

_____

_____

_____

_____

_____

_____

_____

_____

Send out your light and your truth; let them lead me;
let them bring me to your holy hill and to your dwelling.
Psalm 43:3 (ESV)

This beautiful Psalm reminds us that we need to be led. It reminds us that our Father wishes to be just that: our Father. He desires to parent us by guiding us towards that eternal dwelling place. Even though He wishes to be the Light in our lives, however, our God desires that we seek that light. He will not force Himself or His word on anyone. We would do well to pray, as the psalmist prayed, asking God to send his light.

We need to request God's light on a daily, maybe hourly, basis. Our world gives us so many opportunities to turn from God's light that we must be vigilant in our quest to seek out that truth. We must gird our loins with the promise of God's word by reading the Bible daily and seeking a relationship with Christ. We should seek out the company of other Christians to support and encourage one another as we seek that light and then move forward to share this brilliant light with others.

God will provide the light to lead us when we actively pursue that guidance. God will bless our lives when we first seek to bless Him. The brilliance of the light can only be fully appreciated when we are with God in his dwelling, but we can make this earthly world a bit more palatable as we seek out the truth. When we find God's truth we should want to shine as a thanksgiving to God for leading us to his holy hill. We should desire to live as an example of one who is following Christ's light. Do we really want God to send His light? Do we really want the responsibility of being led by God?

Send out your light and your truth; let them lead me;
let them bring me to your holy hill and to your dwelling.
Psalm 43:3 (ESV)

Oh Father God,

Fill me up with the desire to learn Your truth and follow Your Light, O God. Allow me to seek and accept Your teachings and Your plans for my life so that I might reach that eternal resting place. Father, thank You for surrounding me with great Christian folks who keep me turning back to Your light.

_____

_____

_____

_____

_____

_____

_____

_____

_____

_____

_____

Blessed are the people who know the joyful sound!
They walk, O Lord, in the light of Your countenance.
Psalm 89:15 (NKJV)

I sn't this the most glorious scripture? When I close my eyes and listen for that orchestra in heaven, I can see my Lord's precious face. As the light shines behind His shoulder, I can see the strength and the gentleness of my Savior and my Benefactor. I feel that warmth as He pours His love around me and wraps me in the assurance of His promises. It is so easy to hear the joyful sound and see the light of Jesus when I am in my secure place communing with my God.

Then the real world happens. Suddenly I find myself swamped with life, searching for that joyful sound but choosing to hear the horns blasting, music blaring, and the sting of our culture at its worst.

As the Psalmist reminds me, "blessed are the people who know the joyful sound"….and I decide to hear that precious music even in the midst of my world. As I look around, consciously searching for the light of God's face, I see it everywhere. I see Jesus in the troubled student looking for acceptance. I see Jesus in the disheveled young mother paying for groceries with food stamps. I see Jesus in the scared pregnant teen who only wished for love. I see Jesus in the aggressive driver on the interstate as he whizzes past me. I see Jesus in the man as he stands by the graveside of his darling wife. I see Jesus in the nursery holding that infant struggling to breathe.

I hear the joyful sound of Jesus as He shines the light of His beautiful face all over our imperfect world. I hear the joyful sound of Jesus as He loves on all those who find misfortune as they struggle in this imperfect world. I hear the joyful sound of Jesus as He whispers in my ear that we are all children of God and worthy of walking in the light of His countenance. Thank You Jesus!

Blessed are the people who know the joyful sound!
They walk, O Lord, in the light of Your countenance.
Psalm 89:15 (NKJV)

O sweet Jesus,

You are an amazing Savior. Thank You for giving me ears to hear the joyful sound of Your music in this imperfect world. Thank You for shining the light of Your face all over this imperfection so that I might see You at work. You are beautiful and perfect and I am blessed in Your shining light.

_____

_____

_____

_____

_____

_____

_____

_____

_____

_____

_____

Your word is a lamp to guide me and a light for my path.
I will keep my solemn promise to obey your just instructions.
Psalm 119:105-106 (GNT)

How many Bibles do you have in your home? How many of those Bibles do you open on a regular basis? Do you write in them, marking them up as God reveals His word to you? Do you share those words with your family and your friends? Dear friend, do you understand what a precious gift those Bibles are to you and to me?

God, in all His wisdom, gave us His Word in a written form so that we might converse with Him on a regular basis. He knew that we would need an instruction manual for operating in this world and He provided. There is nothing that we have, or will, experience that God did not address in the book of instructions that He handed down to us. He gave us examples of men and women just like us to illustrate the way we are to walk the Christian walk. Our story has already been told in the great Bible characters that have come before us. Best of all, we know the end. We have read the last chapter and know that God wins!

But the Psalmist reminds us that we cannot just read the word, we have to obey it. Ouch! Sometimes that is the hard part. It seems easy to read the text and know what the words say; it is considerably more difficult sometimes to do what the text tells us to do. As a Christian I know that the Bible tells me to love my enemies. Does that really mean that I have to love the man that purposefully hurt my neighbor? Does that really mean that I have to love the gunman who shot the children in that school?

A relationship with our Lord and Savior makes it abundantly clear that all of his instructions are for us to obey, not just the easy ones. However, I believe that when we have a relationship with Christ we desire to read His word and obey His law to please Him. We view abstract ideas like love and hate through the lens of the Bible rather than from the perspective of the world. Reading His word with His lamp shining down on the words gives us a new reality. He has promised to light our path now we must promise to obey.

Your word is a lamp to guide me and a light for my path.
I will keep my solemn promise to obey your just instructions.
Psalm 119:105-106 (GNT)

Father God,

In all Your wisdom, You have given us the source to live this life in a manner that pleases You. Thank You for knowing that we would need Your instruction. Please keep me willing to obey.

_____

_____

_____

_____

_____

_____

_____

_____

_____

_____

_____

_____

The unfolding of Thy words gives light;
It gives understanding to the simple.
-Psalm 119:130 (NASB)

There is nothing like getting up with expectancy in the morning. As God directs the sun to rise and bring a natural light to the world, I get into God's Word and ask Him to direct the light of His Word into my heart of understanding. Over the years as I have begun my day like this, He has never failed to meet me and answer my prayer.

Years ago I went to a Rolling Stones' concert. The concert was to begin at 9:00 PM, and at about five minutes before that time the lights dimmed and the height of anticipation kicked in. To our dismay at five after nine the lights were still low and Mick had not appeared on stage yet. As we waited my heart began to race and I could hardly breathe with the excitement in the air. Finally the lights went up and the Stones came out and I still remember the thrill of it all. For a woman who was normally in bed by 9:00, the night proved to be a very late night with few hours of sleep.

I recall I got up the next morning like always and went into my room where I have my quiet time with the Lord. I remember praying that the Lord would show me the truth in His Word and bring light to my understanding. I will never forget how I was reading in Nehemiah where Ezra was reading the Law before the assembly of the men, women, and all who could listen with understanding. These people evidently were excited about the Word of God. It says they listened from early morning until midday. It goes on to explain the people stood up as He read it. Then they shouted. Then they bowed low and worshiped the Lord.

It immediately broke my heart when I realized I was sitting there tired and with little, if any, excitement at being in the presence of Almighty God, the Creator of the Universe. Why had my heart pounded so the night before in the presence of mere men? That morning God's Word changed my life dramatically. It caused a paradigm shift like I had never experienced before. The Scriptures shed light on an area of my life that needed attention. It exposed how my priorities were out of line.

As painful as that experience was, I thank God that He cares so deeply for me and is willing to shine His light into the dark areas of my life and reveal where I need to change.

The unfolding of Thy words gives light;
It gives understanding to the simple.
-Psalm 119:130 (NASB)

Almighty God, You are the God of Abraham, Ezra, Nehemiah and me. The Word tells me You never change. Stir my heart in such a way that will cause me to awaken in the morning with such an expectancy of meeting with You that I will joyfully get out of bed, excited about what the light of Your Word will reveal to me as I prayerfully study it.

_____

_____

_____

_____

_____

_____

_____

_____

_____

_____

_____

If I say, "Surely the darkness will overwhelm me, and the light around me will be night," even the darkness is not dark to You, and the night is as bright as the day. Darkness and light are alike to You.
Psalm 139:11-12 (NASB)

A s a little girl I was very afraid of the dark. I had a great imagination and conjured up all kinds of supernatural things that could harm me. I never once thought that there was a supernatural being that accompanied me everywhere I went as my Protector. It was not until well into my Christian walk that I discovered Psalm 139 and the truths it held.

God is omniscient, all-seeing, and the dark is no different than the light to Him. He sees everything as clearly in the dark as He does in the light. As dark as the hearts of men are becoming, there is no problem with God seeing them for what they are.

Being a voracious reader, I peruse the Best Seller list quite often. Sometimes I shudder when I see what we are reading and what it says about who we are and what we are becoming. Recently a woman told me she was reading a certain book but kept a book cover over it so her kids and husband wouldn't know what she was reading. I thought about the times we think we can hide things from God, forgetting He sees it all. His vision, unlike ours, is not impaired in the darkness.

If I say, "Surely the darkness will overwhelm me, and the light around me will be night," even the darkness is not dark to You, and the night is as bright as the day. Darkness and light are alike to You.
Psalm 139:11-12 (NASB)

Dear Omniscient One, I am so very thankful that when I am in the dark, You are always there with me and I have nothing to fear. How foolish You must think we are when we seek to hide things from You. We praise You right now for being not just in the light, but the very Light Himself. I give You all my fears right now, knowing that You have made me more than a conqueror.

_____

_____

_____

_____

_____

_____

_____

_____

_____

_____

_____

But the path of the righteous is like the light of dawn,
which shines brighter until full day.
Proverbs 4:18 (ESV)

Have you ever left to go on vacation in the wee hours of the dawn? When our daughters were little we used to pack up the car and leave before 4 AM so the girls would sleep a good bit of the journey. It made long hours of riding along the interstate much easier as our sweet kiddos slumbered in the back seat. It was also a kind of quiet peace for me as my husband and I traveled along the dark roads sipping coffee and watching the day begin.

First light would start to emerge giving just a hint of the outline of the horizon. Shadows replaced blackness and a glimmer of brightness promised a new day would soon be upon us. We could feel the anticipation of the fullness of this new day and we put behind the old as we moved toward our destination. Finally, the sun would pop out and the fullness of the daylight would fill the car causing the girls to begin to stir, hungry and ready for a stop.

I see our Christian walk as following a similar path. We begin our journey all snug and peaceful. We can see the light and know we are moving toward it, but all seems a bit shadowy. We continue to move along the road of life trying to be "good", reading the Bible and going to church. The Light of the Lord is shadowy to us, but we are hopeful that when we have more time we will walk fully with our God. Then suddenly, the full light emerges, as if moved from behind a cloud, and we are enveloped in the radiance in a way that makes us hungry for more of God. We have to stop the rotating door of life and begin building up that relationship with Christ. We find ourselves in the full Light of God and we want to share that warm place with everyone we encounter. We move toward the Light in new and powerful ways and wonder at the splendor of the brightness.

But the path of the righteous is like the light of dawn,
which shines brighter until full day.
Proverbs 4:18 (ESV)

Thank You God for showering us in Your Light. We love that You are traveling with us down the road of life. Thank You for giving us the degree of brightness that we need to move along until suddenly You desire to reveal Your full brilliance to us. Help me to respond to Your light in ways that are pleasing to You and will glorify Your name.

_____

_____

_____

_____

_____

_____

_____

_____

_____

_____

_____

The righteous are like a light shining brightly;
The wicked are like a lamp flickering out.
Proverbs 13:9 (GNT)

The book of Proverbs is full of rich moral teachings that encourage us in everyday, practical kinds of matters. Proverbs 13:9 is no exception. This Scripture tells us that if we are righteous we are to keep that Light of God shining brightly. We call ourselves righteous, but do we really know what that word means?

My Webster's Collegiate Dictionary defines righteous as "acting in accord with divine or moral law; free from guilt or sin." These are the very qualities that God wishes to see in His people that carry the torch for Him. The words make it sound very easy. Real life makes it seem very hard. Lucky for us that God gives us instructions so we know how to carry His light and keep it shining brightly. We read His Word to find out how to deal with every situation we could possibly encounter. His Word allows His People to know how to behave in a righteous manner and since we can be righteous, we then must also take on the job of keeping His light shining brightly.

The Scripture tells us, on the other hand, that the wicked let the lamp flicker out. The dark lifestyle of those living outside of God's directives shroud His light and even, over time, cause the darkness to take over that light. Beloved, we need to be not only righteous for ourselves, but also a righteous example for those whose light is dim. We need to be that tiny dot of light that grows brighter and bolder as the darkness creeps in. We need to shine brightly in those darkest places in the name of our faultless and radiant God.

The righteous are like a light shining brightly;
The wicked are like a lamp flickering out.
Proverbs 13:9 (GNT)

Dear Lord,

Help me to stay on the righteous path and keep my light shining brightly to lead others to You. Give me the desire to be a role model so that others will see the light that I carry and want to know You.

_____

_____

_____

_____

_____

_____

_____

_____

_____

_____

_____

_____

The lamp of the Eternal illuminates the human spirit,
searching our most intimate thoughts.
Proverbs 20:27 (The Voice)

W hat is the lamp of the Eternal? Ask this question and you could get the wrong answer. The better question is – Who is the Lamp of the Eternal? I believe it is the Holy Spirit. He works very much like a flashlight directing light into the deep recesses of our very spirit.

We like the idea of the Lord's light shining on others who have things to hide, or have less-than-good intentions, or those who are just plain evil. After all, they deserve it. We too often relish the idea of people getting what they deserve – until it comes to us.

We, before coming to Christ, deserved death, but by God's amazing grace we have been saved. We still have those areas in our lives that are not as pure as they should be. These are the places the Lamp of the Eternal wants to illuminate in us. Often times our dirtiest areas are not that visible to others, but lie in our intimate thoughts. These are His specialty.

It can be a painful ordeal to earnestly let the Holy Spirit have His way in our lives to the point where He shows us who we really are, but that is part of the refining process. The effect of this is growing in the holiness in which we are exhorted to walk. Another result of the Holy Spirit "cleaning out our closets" is that the dark recesses that are exposed, can be replaced with His light. The more light in our soul, the brighter the light we shine for Christ.

We should quit trying to hide from God. It didn't work for Adam and Eve, and it won't work for us. To be humble is to see oneself as he/she truly is. Let's get real with God, not fearing what the Light may reveal, but humbly coming before His Presence baring our very souls.

The lamp of the Eternal illuminates the human spirit,
searching our most intimate thoughts.
Proverbs 20:27 (The Voice)

Lamp of the Eternal, I sincerely desire You to show me what You find as You search my heart and my intimate thoughts. I know the refiner's fire can be painful, but I long to be a bright reflection of You. Don't allow me to keep any area of my life untouched by Your Light. I pray others will see Your light in me and that my life might bring glory to Your name. Amen.

_____

_____

_____

_____

_____

_____

_____

_____

_____

_____

Then I saw that there is more gain in wisdom than in folly,
as there is more gain in light than in darkness.
Ecclesiastes 2:13 (ESV)

I love God's Word because it makes so much sense. This verse is a great example of the common sense that can be found there. It seems it is a no-brainer that there is more to gain in light than in darkness; however, God sees fit to include it in His Word. God knows something we don't know.

Could it be that many of us are deceived? Has the difference between light and dark been clouded by shades of gray? God's Word is black and white, yet the world insists on gray areas by altering what God has said. After all isn't that exactly what the serpent did in the Garden of Eden? "Has God really said?"

Or could it be that some of us prefer the darkness because it hides our deeds of the flesh? We mistakenly think, because it is hard for us to see in the dark, God has the same problem. The Word tells us that light and dark are the same to Him.

Finally, could it be that we don't realize that the most important gain we get in the light is salvation through Jesus Christ. Philippians tells us in chapter 3:8 More than that, I count all things to be loss in view of the surpassing value of knowing Christ Jesus my Lord, for whom I have suffered the loss of all things, and count them but rubbish so that I may gain Christ. This is why the light is favorable, because the gain is priceless.

> Then I saw that there is more gain in wisdom than in folly,
> as there is more gain in light than in darkness.
> Ecclesiastes 2:13 (ESV)

Lord God, I thank You for Your word and that it is not only practical but also trustworthy. I thank You for the gain in my life because of my relationship with Jesus. Help me to count all else a loss compared to what I have in You. Help me to choose the light over the dark every time. Amen.

_____

_____

_____

_____

_____

_____

_____

_____

_____

_____

_____

_____

Now descendants of Jacob. Let us walk in the light
which the Lord gives us!
Isaiah 2:5 (GNT)

Family name is a powerful thing. Everyone is familiar with certain family names. Kennedy, Lincoln, Hitler: all names that evoke a clear picture or response. What about within our own families? Are you named after someone that came before you or did you name your child after a relative? Many of us take great pride in our names and work hard to maintain the integrity of our family name. Have you thought about the fact that we are all spiritual descendants of Jacob? What a wonderful way to be identified! What a wonderful family name to carry on!

Family names also sometimes bring responsibility. Did your parent ever say to you that you needed to uphold the family name? Were you ever held accountable during your school years when a teacher recognized your name and knew your parent or sibling? We are so mindful of protecting our names and making sure that no blemish is associated with that name. Shouldn't we be equally prudent to guard the name of our descendants in Christ?

As Christians we should boldly proclaim our heritage and work to preserve the reputation that heritage carries with it. One way to do so is to live the message in Isaiah 2:5. We should all "walk in the light" so that the Lord is pleased with us and others look to us as a role model. Our actions really do speak louder than our words so how we go about living our lives is a direct reflection on how people see us as Christians. We all would do well to uphold the name and reputation of the family of Jacob.

Now descendants of Jacob. Let us walk in the light
which the Lord gives us!
Isaiah 2:5 (GNT)

Sweet Father God,

You have given us big shoes to fill in being spiritual descendants of Jacob. Help us to be worthy of that heritage so that we are ever walking in Your Light, Lord. Show us how to uphold that rich reputation and be a light for others.

_____

_____

_____

_____

_____

_____

_____

_____

_____

_____

_____

_____

Woe to those who call evil good, and good evil;
who substitute darkness for light and light for darkness;
who substitute bitter for sweet and sweet for bitter.
Isaiah 5:20 (NASB)

According to this, God would not have us alter the truth. Our plumb line is to be the word of God and what He calls evil is evil, and what He calls darkness is darkness, and bitter is nothing less than bitter. God's word is absolute, and we are to handle it correctly.

Shakespeare wrote that a rose by any other name is still as sweet. This is also true when it comes to our renaming concepts such as evil, dark and bitter. We may call them what we like, but God's word and definitions still remain correct. The problem with exchanging the truth for a lie is that we not only distort the truth, we set ourselves up to be God.

I heard a friend mention she didn't like to call God "Father" because her earthly father wasn't a good father. She was letting man define

God instead of the other way around. We are doing the same when we decide what God calls evil is really good, or darkness is really light.

God's love is what moves His hand toward us. Therefore, it would behoove us to let Him determine what is good and what is light in our lives. Remember it cost Him His only Son to deliver us out of darkness into the light. Let's walk in the light for our own good and as a sacrifice of praise.

Woe to those who call evil good, and good evil;
who substitute darkness for light and light for darkness;
who substitute bitter for sweet and sweet for bitter.
Isaiah 5:20 (NASB)

God, You are the God of Abraham, Isaac, Jacob and me. I thank You that You care enough about me that You are adamant about what I should or should not do. I ask You to search my heart O God and see if there be any wicked way in me and lead me by Your Light everlasting.

_____

_____

_____

_____

_____

_____

_____

_____

_____

_____

_____

The people who walked in darkness have seen a great light
Those who dwelt in the land of the shadow of death,
Upon them a light has shined.
Isaiah 9:2 (NKJV)

I love to camp in state parks. There is such a sense of peace for me when I am in the middle of God's creation with my family, my horse, and my dog. All seems right with the world, until I slip a bit too far from the camp sight and darkness comes rushing in. Suddenly I am alone. I have cut myself off from my loved ones and am too far into the woods to see the home fires burning. When this happens I feel edgy and a bit frightened. I call out for someone to come to me and share his/her flashlight to lead me back to camp.

Sin creeps in on us like this sometimes too. We are in the middle of a lovely life then find ourselves strayed away from the light. Sin has lured us into the woods. We walk in darkness. We can't find the right direction. Because the obstacles are not illuminated we crash right into them head first, and then pick ourselves up only to hit them again. Fear sets in and causes judgment to be marred, and the darkness only becomes thicker.

We so need to cry out to our Savior at these times in our lives. We need to ask our Sovereign Lord to bring His flashlight to lead us back to the comfort of His brilliant light. He so wants to lead us out of the darkness that hovers in the woods. Our Lord desires that we bask in the warmth of His pure light and walk in peace as His children. He shows us the lighted path. We just have to choose to walk it. We need to look for that light and then focus on it solely and head right back to camp. God is that friend who meets us with the flashlight.

David reminds us in Psalms 27, "The Lord is my light and my salvation – whom shall I fear?" (verse 1, Amplified Bible, OT).

The people who walked in darkness have seen a great light
Those who dwelt in the land of the shadow of death,
Upon them a light has shined.
Isaiah 9:2 (NKJV)

Lord God,

I am so sorry when I have strayed from Your light and chosen the darkness over You. Please forgive me when I allow myself to wander rather than staying on the marked trail. Thank You for carrying the shining light so that I might find my way back.

_____

_____

_____

_____

_____

_____

_____

_____

_____

_____

_____

57

I form light and create darkness,
I make well being and create calamity,
I am the Lord, who does all these things.
Isaiah 45:7 (ESV)

This Scripture reminds us that our God is in control of all. Isaiah reads that "He formed light and dark". Wow! Have you ever sat back and marveled at the break of day as the dawn is opening up the sky? Or maybe, you are a sunset watcher. God does an amazing job with His artwork as the sunlight kisses the earth goodnight. How can anyone suggest that our God is not the overseer of such routine clock work. Day and night continue to roll along just as God planned. Man can change clocks and set random time zones, but God will always provide a day and a night for His people.

The Lord also says that He makes well-being and calamity. Sometimes God's people step into the darkness and God, in all His righteousness, must remind us that He is in control. He can choose to bring calamity onto His creation to make a point and get our attention. God does this to encourage His people to repent and turn to Him rather than sin. We would do well to not provoke our God to respond with calamity.

God would prefer to have us walk with Him in the light and allow Him to shower us with well being. In His divine wisdom, God created an order to this world and desires that we step into that place that He designed for us alone. That place in the light.

I form light and create darkness,
I make well being and create calamity,
I am the Lord, who does all these things.
Isaiah 45:7 (ESV)

Thank You dear Father for creating that special place for me, emblazoned by Your mighty hand, in Your heavenly presence. Give me the strength to step into that well-lit path and turn my back on the secular clock so that I might rightfully rest in that place You have provided.

_____

_____

_____

_____

_____

_____

_____

_____

_____

_____

_____

Arise, shine; for your light has come, and the glory of the Lord has risen upon you. For behold, darkness will cover the earth and deep darkness the peoples; But the Lord will rise upon you and His glory will appear upon you. Nations will come to your light, and kings to the brightness of your rising.
Isaiah 60:1-3 (NASB)

This was a promise to God's people. It still applies to God's people. The Light has come in the person of Jesus Christ. His glory appears upon us in the form of the Holy Spirit. There is a light within us that radiates. This is no little light, but one that becomes a beacon that draws others to us.

Have you ever noticed how there are those people who want nothing to do with us while life is going along well? But it happens very often that those are the very ones who seek us out when the world is caving in on them via some tragedy. They see in us something they want. They can't call it by its proper name- God's Light- but they are drawn to it when the darkness is closing in on them.

It would be a grave mistake to deprive the world of the Light within us. We would be robbing the world of a God-given phenomenon. We must remember He is supernatural, so we should not be surprised when the unlikely happens in our lives. We need to be willing to take on the role of a beacon in a very dark world.

Arise, shine; for your light has come, and the glory of the Lord has risen upon you. For behold, darkness will cover the earth and deep darkness the peoples; But the Lord will rise upon you and His glory will appear upon you. Nations will come to your light, and kings to the brightness of your rising.
Isaiah 60:1-3 (NASB)

Almighty God, thank You for placing Your Light within us. We pray we may continue to tell the story of Christmas –God with us-to all we encounter regardless of the seasons. We are told to put on the Lord Jesus. I am thankful He is always in style.
Amen.

I will bear the indignation of the Lord because I have sinned against Him,
until He pleads my cause and executes judgment for me.
He will bring me out to the light; I shall look upon his vindication.
Micah 7:9 (ESV)

This Scripture reminds us that we will all sin. It does not say when I sin, rather it says "I have sinned". The price of any sin is that we disappoint God and put Him in a position to dole out punishment. Our God is a good and just God which means that He must uphold His righteousness. We should expect to be chastised when we are disobedient. If we believe that our God is good, we should realize that He must bring us out to the light. In a secular court of law, those judges that uphold the law and punish disobedience are call "good". How much better then is our heavenly Father? Should we not also call Him "good" when He takes on the role of perfect judge?

But the court case does not end there. You see, our Lord also pleads our case for us. He will not forsake us but will take the power of our sin away. God the judge is also God our Father and will forgive us in the name of Jesus. God becomes our advocate and will bring us into the light so that we might be seen with no blemish and enter into that heavenly kingdom with all the promise of eternity.

Because we all are guilty of sin, but have the cross to look upon in wonder, we know without a shadow of a doubt that our God loves us and will pardon us on that judgment day. We can not escape our just punishment as the law leaves us guilty. However, the Light of Jesus takes that guilt from us and pays our debt in full.

I will bear the indignation of the Lord because I have sinned against Him,
until He pleads my cause and executes judgment for me.
He will bring me out to the light; I shall look upon his vindication.
Micah 7:9 (ESV)

Sweet Jesus,

Thank You for taking on the anguish of the cross. Your love for me is so pure and so complete that I should expect Your displeasure when I fall short of Your will by sinning. Thank You for continuing to love me, even in the midst of those moments that I must be punished for my disobedience. Thank You for quietly leading me back into the light yet again.

_____

_____

_____

_____

_____

_____

_____

_____

_____

_____

You are the light of the world. A city set on a hill cannot be hidden.
Matthew 5:14 (ESV)

In this gospel lesson, Matthew was speaking to the disciples of Jesus reminding them that they had been commissioned for a lofty job. Jesus directed them that they were to spread His light to all. As disciples, their most important duty was to be the light of Jesus. They could not hide that light any more than the brightness of the city might be hidden.

A few years ago my husband and I were traveling along the sand hills in Nebraska. We drove for at least two hours without seeing a house or a light anywhere. As darkness approached we were beginning to feel a bit apprehensive because we were getting very low on diesel fuel and saw no promise of upcoming service stations. Finally, we saw the brightness of a town on the horizon but it was almost a half an hour before we arrived at the outskirts to purchase that badly needed fuel. That city was a sight for sore eyes and in the middle of the darkness, it was one that could not be mistaken. God's light is like that. It is a beacon of hope in the midst of darkness and need.

We should, like those disciples, take the job of being the light very seriously. We need to hold the light high and proudly and shine the way for all. Sometimes that might mean that we have to stand in the middle of the darkness to guide the way for those folks seeking a way. Sometimes that might mean that we stand outside of the darkness and hold the light as a kind of beacon. Always, we must shine the light in the name of our precious savior, Jesus.

You are the light of the world. A city set on a hill cannot be hidden.
Matthew 5:14 (ESV)

Sweet Jesus,

Thank you for giving me Your light and using me to share that light with others. Please keep me true to that task and help me to remember that Your brightness can not be overlooked or hidden.

_____

_____

_____

_____

_____

_____

_____

_____

_____

_____

_____

_____

The eye is the lamp of the body.
If your eyes are good, your whole body will be full of light.
Matthew 6:22 (NIV)

A s I read this verse I can interpret it in various ways. The meaning that is most convicting is the thought that what my eyes behold can penetrate my inner being. It makes me consider: What kinds of things am I looking at? Am I lusting after things of this world? I know one of Satan's tricks he pulled in the Garden of Eden and again with Jesus in the wilderness was appealing to the lust of the eyes. He knows what we see can be the beginning of the process that leads us to sin. David first "saw" Bathsheba. Eve looked and "saw" the fruit was good. The rest is His story.

What about the books and magazines we read? Are we reading things that encourage our walk with the Lord (hopefully right now you are.) Are the stories we enjoy edifying to the body? Are the illustrations causing us to stumble? I think one way to determine if we should be reading certain material is to see if our Spirit is satisfied or our flesh. Naturally the more time we spend in these forms of entertainment the more they can help us or harm us.

Technology is fabulous; I love my Kindle and the internet. However, I would be remiss if I did not mention my concern for the amount of pornography out there and the way social networking has replaced genuine relationships. How many hours are we staring at a computer screen? The flip side to our verse is that if we constantly look upon the darkness, our whole body will be dark. I believe like so many things in the world the darkness can gently erode the light until we are in over our heads before we know it.

We want our whole body to be full of light, so we might be great witnesses for Christ. We want to set a good example for others. The last thing we need is to become myopic people, allowing our near-sightedness to keep us from having an eternal perspective. I am reminded of the song that begins with the words: Turn your eyes upon Jesus, look full in His wonderful face; and the things of this world will grow strangely dim, in the light of His glory and grace.

The eye is the lamp of the body.
If your eyes are good, your whole body will be full of light.
Matthew 6:22 (NIV)

Lord Jesus, help me to keep my focus on Your wonderful face. I want to have an eternal perspective as I walk through this life. I would ask that You would prick my heart when I am gazing on something that is not feeding my Spirit. I pray that the things that break Your heart would break mine. Amen.

_____

_____

_____

_____

_____

_____

_____

_____

_____

_____

_____

"Come to Me, all who are weary and burdened, and I will give you rest. Put My yoke upon your shoulders – it might appear heavy at first, but it is perfectly fitted to your curves. Learn from Me, for I am gentle and humble of heart. When you are yoked to Me, your weary souls will find rest. For My yoke is easy, and My burden is light."
Matt. 11:28-30 (The Voice)

A re you worn out? God would not have us over-tax our bodies and spirits the way we do. It is hard not to encounter someone each day that doesn't express his/her weariness. Generally their comments are followed by some man-made remedy: learn to say no, get more sleep, eat better, prioritize their lives, work less, de-stress, and get organized. Though all these things can benefit us, they are not the answer. Once again, the answer is found in God's word. We need to get yoked with Jesus. This sounds like an interesting platitude, but how it is achieved?

Oxen were yoked to share the burden and to keep in step with each other. The beauty of our Lord is He is willing to take the burden to the point that our share is light. He is willing to walk in a way that we can stay in step with Him, if we are willing to listen to Him. There is no fear in being in step with Jesus, for He is gentle and humble of heart, and only He can perfectly fit the yoke to each one of us. He knows exactly how much we can bear and will not overload us. He knows exactly which way we need to go and will not lead us astray. Finally, the best promise in this passage is we will find rest for our weary souls. This is an eternal rest He promises. Won't you stop trying to go it alone, only armed with your worldly wisdom? Instead get hooked up with Jesus. Let Him take the load off.

"Come to Me, all who are weary and burdened, and I will give you rest. Put My yoke upon your shoulders – it might appear heavy at first, but it is perfectly fitted to your curves. Learn from Me, for I am gentle and humble of heart. When you are yoked to Me, your weary souls will find rest. For My yoke is easy, and My burden is light.
Matt. 11:28-30 (The Voice)

Lord Jesus, I give You my burdens, I lay down my will to allow You to lead me in Your perfect path for my life. I relish the idea of being in step with You while You offer me a much needed rest. It only makes sense that You would offer a burden which is light to those who walk in Your light. I love you, Lord. It is in Your precious name I pray. Amen.

Now after the Sabbath, toward the dawn of the first day of the week, Mary Magdalene and the other Mary went to see the tomb. And behold, there was a great earthquake, for an angel of the Lord descended from heaven and came and rolled back the stone and sat on it. His appearance was like lightning, and his clothing white as snow. And for fear of him the guards trembled and became like dead men. But the angel said to the women, "Do not be afraid, for I know that you seek Jesus who was crucified. He is not here, for he has risen, as he said. Come, see the place where He lay."
Matthew 28:1-6 (ESV)

This dawning of the first day of the week was no ordinary sunrise. It followed the darkest three days of all history. It followed a time when Satan had thought he had won. It followed the slaying of the Passover lambs. It followed the death of a would-be King. It followed the burial of a mother's son. The brightest light seems to always follow the darkest hour. This was the epitome of that truth.

What no one understood was that this sunrise also followed the rising of the Son. The very Son of God conquered death. In that death He paid a debt we could not pay. For the wages of sin is death. By His stripes we were healed, and in that healing our sins that were like scarlet were made white as snow.

Jesus said that He was the Light of the World. When we begin to understand what was at stake as He lay in that tomb, we begin to comprehend just how close we came to being overtaken by the darkness. But God, in His infinite wisdom had a plan that this particular sunrise was ushering in much more than a new day – instead a new era that would redefine man's eternity. This was the fulfillment of all God's promises. No greater Light has ever shone. Only Jesus can be called The Light of the World.

Now after the Sabbath, toward the dawn of the first day of the week, Mary Magdalene and the other Mary went to see the tomb. And behold, there was a great earthquake, for an angel of the Lord descended from heaven and came and rolled back the stone and sat on it. His appearance was like lightning, and his clothing white as snow. And for fear of him the guards trembled and became like dead men. But the angel said to the women, "Do not be afraid, for I know that you seek Jesus who was crucified. He is not here, for he has risen, as he said. Come, see the place where he lay."
Matthew 28:1-6 (ESV)

Jesus, the Light of my Life and the Light of the World, I love You. I will never be able to express my gratitude for what You did for me on the cross at Calvary. I pray that I might get a glimpse of Your light and that it might ignite my heart for others. I want to reflect Your light into the dark places of my world. Remind me every time I see a sunrise of the Good News that accompanied that dawn that changed the world following Your resurrection.

_____

_____

_____

_____

_____

_____

_____

_____

He said to them, "Is a lamp brought in to be put under the'
bushel basket or under the bed, and not on the lamp stand?"
For there is nothing hidden, except to be disclosed;
nor is anything secret, except to come to light.
Mark 4:21-22 (NRSV)

This gospel message speaks to all of us about the power of God's light. We would do well to remember that His light pierces all darkness. Everything will be disclosed by that brilliance when we come face to face with our God. Don't think for one minute that you can fool God!

Many times we shine for God. We walk the walk and talk the talk, and we are sure that people can know we are Christians. At these times God's Light shines through us and glows around all that we encounter. We are doing well at sharing that light and using it to warm others. God is pleased when His Light is shining brilliantly through His people.

Other times we extinguish God's lamp; maybe even for just a moment. It is then that we become dark and cold. We behave in ways that make people question if we are Christian and know that if we are, they want no part of that. When we hide God's Light we are far from where we should be, but even worse, God knows it. He is saddened by our desire to put out the light, even for the briefest of moments. We may think that we are masked in the darkness, but God knows our heart and mind. There are no secrets kept from God.

Let's work hard to carry the torch and light up our communities; maybe just for today. Can we make the difference in our families, in our workplaces? You bet we can! With God's help, we can be the ones that spread that Light into the darkest corners of our lives. We can be the ones who decide to not hide the lamp, but carry it high and proudly. We can be the ones who splash patches of light on all those around us. We can be the ones that bring a little bit of God's Light into this fallen world.

He said to them, "Is a lamp brought in to be put under the'
bushel basket or under the bed, and not on the lamp stand?"
For there is nothing hidden, except to be disclosed;
nor is anything secret, except to come to light.
Mark 4:21-22 (NRSV)

Dear Father in heaven,

Thank You for reminding us that nothing is hidden from You. It is so easy to fall into the trap of believing that we can step into and out of the light. Keep us mindful of the fact that we need to bring Your light into our lives and let it shine so we are not tempted to slip away. Keep me honest with You so that You might use my light to light the path of another.

_____

_____

_____

_____

_____

_____

_____

_____

_____

Before time itself was measured, the Voice was speaking. The Voice was and
is God. This celestial Word remained ever present with the Creator; His
speech shaped the entire cosmos. Immersed in the practice of creating, all
things that exist were birthed in Him. His breath filled all things with a
living, breathing light – A light that thrives in the depths of darkness, blazes
through murky bottoms. It cannot and will not be quenched.
John 1:1-5 (The Voice)

D o you hear the power and the force in that "breathing light"? He is the living Voice. Have you been to the murky bottoms? Do you feel like you are ensconced in the darkness? There is One who cannot only find you there, but also can rescue you. He is no stranger to the darkness; that is where He has found every single sinner at the moment he or she has called out to Him to be saved.

Many Christians can't remember when they received Jesus as their Savior; they feel like they have always known the Lord. Some of us, however, remember what it was like to feel like we were not only in the dark, but also that there was no way out. Sin reigned in our lives and death was imminent. The darkness was no match for Jesus Christ. Once He came into our lives He has led us into the light. The light provides a new way of life for us.

Because we have been filled with his living, breathing Light, there is no need to be afraid of the dark any longer. The darkness does not have to overcome us. There is a day coming when the light of the Lord will be the only light required to light all existence. In the meantime He has equipped us to say "no" to the deeds of the dark and "yes" to Lord of Light.

Before time itself was measured, the Voice was speaking. The Voice was and is God. This celestial Word remained ever present with the Creator; His speech shaped the entire cosmos. Immersed in the practice of creating, all things that exist were birthed in Him. His breath filled all things with a living, breathing light – A light that thrives in the depths of darkness, blazes through murky bottoms. It cannot and will not be quenched.
John 1:1-5 (The Voice)

Lord Jesus, we are so thankful that You rescued us from the darkness, never to return. We pray that not only will Your light shine in our lives, but Your light in us will illuminate our little corner of the world. You are the Light of the World and in You there is no darkness. Amen.

There was the true Light which, coming into the world,
enlightens every man.
John 1:9 (NASB)

This verse follows several describing that John (who we know as John the Baptist) had come to testify about the Light coming into the world. The gospel wants to make sure we understand that John is not the Light, so we come to verse 9 and it refers to Jesus as the true Light. The wording in the verse uses the definite article "the" indicating there isn't just any light, but "the" one and only true Light. This is the same kind of wording Jesus uses when He refers to Himself as **the** Way, **the** Truth, and **the** Life.

It is so important that we understand there are not various ways for us to follow or various lights to enlighten us. Only Jesus, the Christ, is able to enlighten every man. In this day when the word tolerance has become a word that translates into accepting everyone, it is imperative we understand God, the Father, will not tolerate any other way to Himself than through His only begotten Son.

Jesus was the only One who could satisfy our Holy God, and His sacrificial death was enough to cover every man. Anyone who will receive Him will be enlightened and on the way to the Father.

There was the true Light which, coming into the world,
enlightens every man.
John 1:9 (NASB)

Heavenly Father, forgive us when we, in the name of tolerance, compromise Your absolutes. We recognize Jesus, Your only begotten son, as the one and only true Light. Amen.

_____

_____

_____

_____

_____

_____

_____

_____

_____

_____

_____

_____

_____

Why does God allow for judgment and condemnation? Because the Light, sent from God, pierced through the world's darkness to expose ill motives, hatred, gossip, greed, violence, and the like. Still some people preferred the darkness over the light because their actions were dark.
John 3:19 (The Voice)

The Greek word for light is *phos*: to shine or make manifest. Often times in God's word it is used as a metaphor for good or right behavior as opposed to the deeds of the dark. The Bible does not talk of any shades of gray or gray areas in our behavior. Instead God's word purports absolutes such as righteousness, justice, truth, and goodness. They stand in direct opposition to unrighteousness, injustice, lies, and violence. In the beginning God separated the light from the darkness. The Hebrew word for separated in this passage means to sever utterly. They are not opposite ends of a continuum. There is no happy medium in which to reside. They are meant to be completely and distinctly separate.

For a Christian to find himself with one foot in the light and one foot in the dark, translates into being a hypocrite. As the Scriptures say: the light exposes the deeds of the dark. This is still the reason some reject the Light, for fear their true nature will be seen.

Jesus died, taking all the sins, or deeds of darkness, upon Himself, so we might no longer have to find ourselves teetering back and forth between the light and the dark. Once we come to know our glorious Savior we yearn for the Light to show us the way and yes, even illuminate those times the old nature rears its ugly head. For we know that once our sins are exposed, we can confess them and He is faithful and just to forgive them and cleanse us from all unrighteousness. There is no longer a need to run from the Light.

Why does God allow for judgment and condemnation? Because the Light, sent from God, pierced through the world's darkness to expose ill motives, hatred, gossip, greed, violence, and the like. Still some people preferred the darkness over the light because their actions were dark.
John 3:19 (The Voice)

Light of the World and Light of my life, I pray You would shine Your light on my heart and expose any wicked way in me. Father, I am so thankful that You make it clear in Your word that the light and the dark are not to abide in the same place. If You catch me teetering between the two please extend Your mighty hand and pull me back on Your path and help me walk in the Light. Amen

_____

_____

_____

_____

_____

_____

_____

_____

_____

_____

He was the burning and shining lamp and you were
willing for a time to rejoice in his lamp.
John 5:35 (NKJV)

In this gospel message, Jesus is talking about John the Baptist as a witness who bears testimony to Jesus himself. Jesus calls John a lamp; a lamp that many were willing to listen to and believe. Note that although John was a powerful influence to the people that he ministered to, he was not the Light that we see in Christ Jesus.

This makes me think about when we are camping. After dark I sometimes have to leave the camper to tend to horses and I grab a flashlight on my way out the door to see my way. Yes, the light points out a path so that I do not stumble and fall on the rough terrain, but it is not bright enough for me to clearly see all that I need to adequately care for my horses. I have to step in close to check that water buckets are full and horses are securely tied. Then as I move back toward the camper, the light from within begins to shine brighter. When I open the door and step inside, I turn off the flashlight as the camper is brightly lit and I can see clearly.

John the Baptist might be the flashlight. He certainly provides a lighted path and a direction for our journey, but we need to find the brightness of our Savior's light to see everything with the clarity that God intends. Friend, we must not settle for the flashlight. Even though it sheds a little light, we are created to seek the full brilliant Light of God.

He was the burning and shining lamp and you were
willing for a time to rejoice in his lamp.
John 5:35 (NKJV)

Sweet Jesus,

Thank You for sending John the Baptist to witness for You and shine the path for us to follow right to Your shining light. We love that You knew we needed a guide to lead us to You. Keep us ever seeking to move back into that light when we take the flashlight and go out into our journeys in this life.

_____

_____

_____

_____

_____

_____

_____

_____

_____

_____

Jesus spoke to the Pharisees again. "I am the light of the world," he said.
"Whoever follows me will have the light of life and
will never walk in darkness."
John 8:12 (GNT)

The Pharisees had been challenging Jesus repeatedly about who He was and who He said He was. Jesus never backed down. Over and over Jesus contended that He was the Light, but these learned men of religion continued to doubt. They accused our Savior of blasphemy and mocked and ridiculed Him. However, Jesus was steadfast in His stand that He would lead His people out of darkness.

Sadly, we are often no better than those Pharisees from long ago. When we turn our backs on Jesus, we too are mocking and ridiculing him. We choose to walk in the darkness rather than following Him into that "light of life". We have head knowledge of our Lord, much like the Pharisees, but we do not make the effort or commitment to create heart knowledge of Him. We may not consciously pick the dark path, but sometimes we do not want to follow Jesus because we think that His path is too hard or too boring or too "churchy".

Jesus promises us that if we follow Him we will never be in the dark again. That sounds like a fabulous place to be to me. It seems that this is one choice that only has one real option. Friends, let's turn around right now and begin that journey in Jesus' shadow as He leads us along His light.

> Jesus spoke to the Pharisees again. "I am the light of the world," he said.
> "Whoever follows me will have the light of life and will
> never walk in darkness."
> John 8:12 (GNT)

Sweet Jesus,

Thank You for keeping that light shining even when we turn our back on You. Thank You for being so patient and loving that You slow down so that we might catch up and follow You back into the light. Help me to decide not to walk in the darkness.

_____

_____

_____

_____

_____

_____

_____

_____

_____

_____

_____

So Jesus said to them, "for a little while longer the Light is among you. Walk while you have the Light, so that darkness will not overtake you; he who walks in the darkness does not know where he goes." "While you have the Light, believe in the Light, so that you may become sons of Light."
John 12:35-36 (NASB)

J esus was speaking to His followers. We, as Christians in the 21st century have a distinct advantage over His listeners: the Light is not just with us for a while longer; He is with us and in us. We are reminded throughout the Word of God that we are the temple of the Holy Spirit and that enables us to not only walk in the Light but share the Light with others.

Jesus was encouraging His disciples to take advantage of His being with them. He indicated if they were to walk in the Light, they would not be overtaken by the darkness. What an incredible promise we find in the Scriptures. As the Holy Spirit resides within us we find we no longer have any excuse to be in the dark. This may not seem as a huge deal unless you have had the unfortunate experience of groping about in the dark.

Finally, Jesus mentions there is a belief in the Light that results in becoming sons of Light. This reminds us that this is not a religion but a relationship. As we embrace the Light we embrace brothers and sisters in the body of Christ. Together as we walk in the Light, we should be able to easily illuminate the entire world. Let's eradicate the darkness by becoming one in the Light of the Lord.

So Jesus said to them, "for a little while longer the Light is among you. Walk while you have the Light, so that darkness will not overtake you; he who walks in the darkness does not know where he goes." "While you have the Light, believe in the Light, so that you may become sons of Light."
John 12:35-36 (NASB)

Light of our life, Jesus, we claim Your promise that the darkness will not overtake us. We believe You when You tell us that He who is within us is greater than he who is in the world. We long to walk in Your Light until the very last person in the dark sees his way out. Amen.

_____

_____

_____

_____

_____

_____

_____

_____

_____

_____

_____

It will be your mission (Saul) to open their eyes so that they may turn from darkness to light and from the kingdom of Satan to the kingdom of God.
Acts 26:18 (The Voice)

Wow! What a mission! I must admit as much as I am aware of the importance of evangelism, I never really saw the magnitude and scope quite as clearly as I do in this Scripture. The other thing that I realized from this passage is to what extent God sees our potential when He calls us.

Face it, any way you read this you can't miss the truth of Saul being a brand new Christian, albeit he was an impressive Jewish leader. Frankly, I would have been wary, as many were, with entrusting God's kingdom to the likes of Saul. This incident Paul is recounting to King Agrippa was not all that long after Saul had witnessed and supported Stephen's stoning.

Are we up for the challenge as we walk this Christian walk? Do we see the weightiness of the matter of helping one open his/her eyes? More importantly, do we realize sharing our faith with others has the power to lead someone from one kingdom into another? This is our mission, if we choose to accept it.

God knows our past when He calls us. We can no longer use our past as excuse to not heed His call. The Psalmist at one point pleads with God to "not remember the sins of his youth." No worries there. In Christ we are a new creation.

It will be your mission (Saul) to open their eyes so that they may turn from darkness to light and from the kingdom of Satan to the kingdom of God.
Acts 26:18 (The Voice)

Lord, I now realize what a privilege it is to have You entrust me with helping to open the eyes of one who may or may not be searching for You. It is with humility I choose to accept this mission and pray I might be an instrument of Your love as I endeavor to reach out to those still walking in the darkness, subjects in Satan's kingdom. Amen

_____

_____

_____

_____

_____

_____

_____

_____

_____

_____

_____

The night is far gone; the day is at hand. So then let us cast off the works of darkness and put on the armor of light.
Romans 13:12. (ESV)

In Scriptures we are instructed to perform several duties in the light such as: walking, working, witnessing, and in this verse – warring. Armor is a protective device and just as Ephesians tells us to take up the shield of faith to extinguish the flaming darts of the devil, this verse found in Romans indicates the armor of light will dispel the deeds of darkness.

I know for years I tried in my Christian walk to be a better person in my own strength, and failed every time. Ephesians 6:12 tells us that our struggle is not against flesh and blood, but against the rulers, against the powers, against the world forces of this darkness, and against the spiritual forces of wickedness in the heavenly places. As we take up our light against the darkness, we must understand that this is a spiritual battle in which we find ourselves. Understanding this can make all the difference in the world.

It seems the longer we have walked with the Lord, the quicker we see the darkness approaching us and recognize it for what it truly is. I believe it is a tactic of Satan's to destroy us. His deeds are best accomplished in the dark, whereas ours are accomplished in the light shone forth by the Holy Spirit that is dwelling within us.

When God gives us His Holy Spirit He gives us all we need to overcome the darkness. We are no longer slaves to the darkness, but we are bond-servants to Jesus Christ, the Light of the World.

The night is far gone; the day is at hand. So then let us cast off the works of
darkness and put on the armor of light.
Romans 13:12. (ESV)

Jesus, our Light and our Life, we thank You and praise You for having
paid the wages of our sins. Darkness sought to overtake You, but You
mastered it instead. Remind me as long as I walk and war in Your
Light, I will be victorious. In Your precious name I pray – Amen.

Therefore do not go on passing judgment before the time, but wait until the
Lord comes who will both bring to light the things hidden in the darkness
and disclose the motives of men's hearts; and then each man's praise will
come to him from God.
I Cor. 4:5 (NASB)

When I think of a bright light, I think of a flashlight I
bought my husband one Christmas. It was listed as
having a million candles. If I am not mistaken it was
illegal to shine in certain places due to the brightness. I can't imagine
anything any brighter, but God's word tells me there is a Light from
the Lord that can show things hidden in the darkness and even the
motives of our hearts. That can be either very comforting or a little
scary.

Most of us have become very adept at playing the "hide behind a
mask" game. We base many of our decisions on how "it will look to
others". God is not to be fooled by our charades. He is able to look to
the very heart of the matter, which is where our motives reside.

Deceitful people will find this very disheartening; however, those of us who are Christians should find great joy in this. First of all, He sees the wicked ways of our hearts and still is madly in love with us. Secondly, the only way we can hope to change for the better is to have our dark places (motives) exposed. And finally, there is such freedom that comes with understanding that He knows it all and we don't have to hide behind a mask anymore. We can be who we were meant to be.

I am afraid that when I get to heaven and stand before the Lord, my impure motives will be an area that will be brought to light. There is no point in trying to hide them from God, so we might as well confess them to Him, so He can cleanse us from all unrighteousness and we can experience that abundant life we are promised in His word.

Therefore do not go on passing judgment before the time, but wait until the
Lord comes who will both bring to light the things hidden in the darkness
and disclose the motives of men's hearts; and then each man's praise will
come to him from God.
I Cor. 4:5 (NASB)

Almighty God, the One who sees me as I really am, thank You for still
loving me in-spite of myself. Thank You for caring enough to not
allow me to continue to operate on impure motives. Please continue to
reveal the impure motives of my heart and lead me by Your light in the
right direction. Amen.

_____

_____

_____

_____

_____

_____

_____

_____

_____

_____

The God who spoke light into existence, saying, "Let light shine from the darkness," is the very One who sets our hearts ablaze to shed light on the knowledge of God's glory revealed in the face of Jesus, the Anointed One.
II Corinthians 4:6 (The Voice)

I s your heart ablaze? Are you on fire for God? The two men on the road to Emmaus, after walking with the Lord, asked, "Were not our hearts burning within us while He was speaking to us on the road, while He was explaining the Scriptures to us?" That would have been some Bible study, listening to the Lord expound the Scriptures! But we have His Holy Spirit within us teaching us the Scriptures as we study. If we want our hearts to be ablaze, we need to spend time getting to know our Savior. We need to sit at His feet and listen to His Voice. We need to seek Him in prayer. These encounters with Almighty God cannot help but spark a fire in our hearts.

I am convinced that it is impossible to have an authentic encounter with Jesus and come away no different than before the encounter. Search the Scriptures; see if this is not the case. His light will either kindle your heart's ember or it will reveal the true nature within you and expose the darkness.

Once our hearts are ablaze, our commission is to shed light on the knowledge of God's glory. And where is that glory to be found? We find it in the very face of Jesus Christ, the Anointed One. This is a high calling we have. This calling carries with it the weight of eternity. There is nothing more important we will ever do than shed light on the knowledge of God's glory to this fallen world.

The God who spoke light into existence, saying, "Let light shine from the darkness," is the very One who sets our hearts ablaze to shed light on the knowledge of God's glory revealed in the face of Jesus, the Anointed One.
II Corinthians 4:6 (The Voice)

Heavenly Father, Giver of Light, we long to see Your glory in the face of our Lord. Moses asked you, Father, to show him Your glory. The answer came in the man of Jesus Christ. Ignite our hearts, we pray.

_____

_____

_____

_____

_____

_____

_____

_____

_____

_____

_____

_____

_____

For you were formerly darkness, but now you are Light in the Lord,
walk as children of Light.
Ephesians 5:8 (NASB)

Growing up I was famous for name dropping. Usually the name I dropped was my father's. He was well-known in the community and was very well-liked. I absolutely loved being referred to as Ralph Simms's daughter. During my teenage years I remember my mother telling me one day I was not behaving like a daughter should, and I was giving Daddy a bad name. Even as ornery as I was, I couldn't bear the idea of hurting Daddy's good name.

Now that I bear the name of Christ, in calling myself a Christian, I am even more sensitive to the idea of giving my Father in heaven a bad name. There are days though that I fail to walk as a child of the Light. When that happens, my students and co-workers can't distinguish me from the rest of the world. It is those days I am so ashamed of myself.

People who witness my behavior on those days may draw one of two conclusions: 1) I talk the talk but can't walk the walk, which makes me a hypocrite; or 2) Christ wasn't able to make a new creation out of the old person I was. The latter idea is what breaks my heart and makes me so ashamed. After what Jesus did for me on the cross in order that I might become that daughter of the King, I should be ever diligent in making sure I reflect the light and the love of the Lord in everything I do. I must remember if anyone is in Christ, he/she is a new creation; the old things passed away, behold, new things have come.

For you were formerly darkness, but now you are Light in the Lord,
walk as children of Light.
Ephesians 5:8 (NASB)

Lord Jesus, I confess I too often forget I am a new creation and am to always walk in the light. I can no longer hide behind the excuse that I can't help it. I know Your Holy Spirit can and will enable me to truly represent my Father and His good name. Thank you Jesus and it is in Your name I pray.

_____

_____

_____

_____

_____

_____

_____

_____

_____

_____

_____

That you may show yourselves to be blameless,
innocent, children of God without blemish in the midst
of a crooked and wicked generation, among whom
you are seen as bright lights in the world.
Philippians 2:15 (Amplified Bible, NT)

D o you ever wonder what your purpose is for this life? Do you ever wonder if you are really making any difference? Maybe you work hard to do the right Christian thing. Is it really worth it? Life is hard and being a Christian in this life is even harder. Have you ever been tempted to let someone else hold the torch for Christianity? It would be so easy to step right outside the perimeter of that glow from Christ's light into the dimness for just a short bit. It is easy to justify that you don't intend to stay there in the darkness but just rest there for a while. We all need a break, right? What will it hurt for just a little while?

God's Word tells us that we are to be "without blemish in the midst" of the wickedness in our culture. God wants us to be seen as the "bright light in this world." As Christians, we have a responsibility to shine brightly against the sin and corruption in our world. We should take a stand against all that dims the light of our Savior, Jesus Christ. We should be sending strobe light beams into the shadows everywhere we go, filling up the dark crevices with the light of God. Isaiah put it like this: "the people who walked in darkness have seen a great Light; those who dwelt in the land of intense darkness and the shadow of death, upon then has the Light shined" (Isaiah 9:2 Amplified Bible, OT). God calls the Christians in this world to be that light. Christians are to take up the light and let it shine upon the wicked so that they too might absorb and live within that salvation of Light. Where are the Christians? Sisters and brothers, we are those Christians who carry the Light.

What is my purpose in this life? God calls us all, as His sons and daughters, to be the torch bearers of His Light. We are to bring His Light to the wicked, and we must be about the business of doing that every day of the week. Carrying the torch is not a Sunday activity or an activity for days that are not too busy or when we feel really happy. Carrying the torch is an activity for work days and play days, for hectic days and for stressful days. Carrying the torch is for days full of everyday people doing everyday things and for days that are just plain ugly. Our torch needs to be held higher and shine brighter when life is wicked and cruel so that God's Light can shine into the bleak darkness of the world and reveal truth and love.

That you may show yourselves to be blameless,
innocent, children of God without blemish in the midst
of a crooked and wicked generation, among whom
you are seen as bright lights in the world.
Philippians 2:15 (Amplified Bible, NT)

Sweet Jesus,

Show me how to shine brightly for You. Remind me that my job is to carry Your torch so that others will see the wickedness and choose the Light. Please take hold of my arm and help me raise that torch high so that everyone can experience the brightness of Your Light every day.

Thank you, Father, as You have made us eligible to receive our portion of the inheritance given to all those set apart by the light. You have rescued us from the dark powers and brought us safely into the kingdom of Your Son, whom You love and in whom we are redeemed and forgiven of our sins (through His blood).
Colossians 1:12 (The Voice)

Just what is our portion of the inheritance given to us who are set apart by the light? I remember as a child being very selective when it came to picking a portion of anything –(chocolate: huge portion; spinach: not so huge). When I split something with a friend, I generally wanted the lion's share. How generous is our Father when He makes us eligible to receive our portion of the inheritance?

One of the beautiful things about our Father is He never acts out of character. He is so very good to us in everything He does for us, and He is no different when handing out our portion of the inheritance. He once again gives us the very best: Himself. We read in Psalm 119:57 the LORD is my portion. How can we top that? We can't!

Let's not be content to just be saved, but let's have that abundant life the Word promises us. Let's stake our claim to our full inheritance, obtaining everything afforded us in Christ Jesus. Let's agree with the psalmist – the Lord is my portion, I need nothing else.

Thank you, Father, as You have made us eligible to receive our portion of the inheritance given to all those set apart by the light. You have rescued us from the dark powers and brought us safely into the kingdom of Your Son, whom You love and in whom we are redeemed and forgiven of our sins (through His blood).
Colossians 1:12 (The Voice)

Almighty God, my Father, I thank You for being such a good god, One who gives His children only the very best. In You I am one of the richest people I know. My inheritance is even more than the lion's share; it is all I will ever need or want. Your generosity is beyond my comprehension. Take the selfish nature out of me as I seek to be worthy of the gifts You have given me. Amen.

_____

_____

_____

_____

_____

_____

_____

_____

_____

_____

But you, beloved, are not in darkness,
for that day to surprise you like a thief;
For you are all children of light and children of the day;
we are not of the night or darkness"
I Thessalonians 5:4-5 (NRSV)

Paul wrote these words to his brothers and sisters in the Thessalonian church to encourage them to persevere in their quest to walk in God's Light. These people were beginning to waver in their daily practices. They were tempted to turn to the dark and Paul felt compelled to remind them that they "belong to the day" (5:8).

How I wish that Paul were here today to share these heartfelt words with those of us who find ourselves in that dark place between sinful darkness and our Savior's healing Light. It is so easy to fall into the temptation that the thief of the night holds out to us. Some will justify inappropriate lifestyles and actions believing that there is time to repent later. Our culture encourages folks to live now and beg forgiveness later. We have become Sunday Christians who devoutly attend church and Bible study while we tippy toe into the darker side of contemporary society when no one is looking.

Paul reminds us that we are "children of light". We know the desires of God's heart for our lives and should encourage and strengthen one another. We need to stand tall in the Light of our Redeemer and hold the hand of those beside us to broaden the circle of His Light. "For God has destined us not for wrath but for obtaining salvation through our Lord Jesus Christ." (5:9) I am reminded that God desires salvation for all of us, but if we do not continue to prepare for the glorious moment when we will be reunited with our Lord, we may find ourselves surprised. We lock the doors of our homes against the burglar and leave the light on to discourage his entrance, but we leave our minds and our hearts so vulnerable against the darkness of sin.

In order to keep the Light of Jesus Christ shining brightly in our hearts we must replace the "bulbs" by praying, reading the Bible and standing hand in hand with other Christians. We are children of the Light and we must hold tightly to that heritage and shine brightly for each other and for God.

But you, beloved, are not in darkness,
for that day to surprise you like a thief;
For you are all children of light and children of the day;
we are not of the night or darkness"
I Thessalonians 5:4-5 (NRSV)

Father of the Light,

Thank You for giving me the privilege of shining for You. Help me to stay in the light and to turn my back on the darkness. Remind me to reach out to my brothers and sisters to find strength as we beam Your Light into the darkness of our world.

_____

_____

_____

_____

_____

_____

_____

_____

_____

_____

Who alone has immortality, who dwells in unapproachable light,
whom no one has ever seen or can see.
To Him be honor and eternal dominion. Amen
I Timothy 6:16 (ESV)

Through the letter written to Timothy by the apostle Paul, we get a glimpse of the power and glory of our God. Timothy was faithfully trying to raise up the church in Ephesus and had many that opposed his work and his teachings. In order to lift Timothy up and encourage him to persevere, Paul wrote to him to keep fighting that fight of faith.

Paul reminded Timothy that our King is on the throne and that He alone is all who matters in the walk through life. In His majesty, we can put all our opponents in proper perspective. God's immense glory should bring a sense of smallness to those who are against us. One day we, along side Timothy, will stand before our God in awe and know that our labor was not in vain.

Paul calls God the "King of Kings and Lord of Lords" (vs 15). Nobody or no thing can measure up against our God. If we are working for God, even in the midst of ridicule, He is still God. No matter the opposition; no matter the situation or cruel man; no matter the circumstance, our God still reigns! Our God is bigger than all that can touch us on this earth and in the end He wins! Wow! What an awesome revelation. It reminds me of the words of a song that go something like this "our God is bigger, our God is better, our God is higher than any other".

Who alone has immortality, who dwells in unapproachable light,
whom no one has ever seen or can see.
To Him be honor and eternal dominion. Amen
I Timothy 6:16 (ESV)

Dear God, the King,

You are bigger and better than any other. Take the fear of my enemies from me and replace it with a desire to persevere in this life with the goal to glorify You so that in the end I will be able to approach that light and know that I have pleased You. Amen.

_____

_____

_____

_____

_____

_____

_____

_____

_____

_____

_____

But you are a chosen generation, a royal priesthood, a holy nation,
His own special people, that you may proclaim the praises of Him
who called you out of darkness into His marvelous light.
1 Peter 2:9 (NKJV)

G od chose me and God chose you! Doesn't that make you want to stand a little straighter and put a smile on your face? We all want to be chosen; to be singled out as special and important. It is kind of like back in elementary school when you were chosen to be on the dodge ball team. Yes! Somebody wants me to stand along side them because they think I will help the cause. As a child, we might have been picked because we were good at throwing the ball, or maybe really fast, or maybe just because the captain liked us. God chose us just because we are His!

When God declared that we were a "chosen generation" He sifted us out of the darkness and in doing so, gave us a responsibility to act like royalty. We can no longer wallow in the sin of this world but must behave in ways that portray our heritage. Christians, God's special people, are called to reflect the light of God. How do we do that? By taking on the words from Scripture and following Jesus' example. We must find in our heart ways to exemplify God's perfect love to all we encounter. We must be true to ourselves and true to our God. We must proclaim God's holy name and spread His light everywhere.

Knowing that God chose me, that He wanted me on his team, makes me want to work a little harder to win the game for Him. Knowing that God has the confidence that I can play this game to perfection makes me want to excel and bring others along with me. God gave me the crown to wear so that I might be a role model for others on the team. Won't you join me? Won't you step into God's light and take your place as a chosen one?

But you are a chosen generation, a royal priesthood, a holy nation,
His own special people, that you may proclaim the praises of Him
who called you out of darkness into His marvelous light.
1 Peter 2:9 (NKJV)

Oh God Almighty,

You are awesome and perfect in every way. You have given me this place on Your team and given me the title of chosen one, now help me clearly see the game plan so that I might bring glory to You. Give me opportunities to share Your light with others so that they too might wish to be on Your team.

_____

_____

_____

_____

_____

_____

_____

_____

_____

_____

_____

Every good and perfect gift is from above, coming down from the Father of the heavenly lights, who does not change like shifting shadows.
James 1:17 (NIV)

J ust what are these heavenly lights? Are they indeed the children of our heavenly Father? I too often think of them as mere stars; then I am reminded of a star that led the magi to the babe who would change the world. Children obey their fathers, and as we read the Scriptures we find that this star appeared, disappeared and reappeared. I can't think of any reason other than the Father of the heavenly lights commanded it. In obedience, that star reacted.

Do we have an explanation for why the sun rises every morning? How do the planets and the other heavenly orbs stay in orbit or even in the sky? Are we so naïve that we believe it is just by coincidence or happenstance?

Looking more closely at the Father of the heavenly lights, we see that He is indeed a good Father, for the gifts He gives are good and perfect. His gifts are irrevocable; we are told in His word. I think the latter portion of our verse in James indicates why these gifts are not taken away or back: He does not change.

As a mom, I cannot say the same about me. There were times I would give things to my kids and then threaten to take them away if they misbehaved. Isn't it wonderful to know that our Father, the Father of the heavenly lights, is One who can be totally relied upon. We don't ever have to wonder how He will react to our circumstances. These aforementioned shifting shadows we certainly can relate to. Depending on time of day or the direction in which we find ourselves these shadows can wax and wane. Not so our Father of heavenly lights. He is the same yesterday, today and forever. How comforting!!

Every good and perfect gift is from above, coming down from the Father of
the heavenly lights, who does not change like shifting shadows.
James 1:17 (NIV)

Dear Father of the heavenly lights, we acknowledge that You are the
One who created the heavens and the earth. Creator God teach me how
to rely upon Your steadfastness, Your faithfulness, and Your
unchanging Love. I want to obey You on a daily basis as the stars in
the heavens do. Amen.

_____

_____

_____

_____

_____

_____

_____

_____

_____

_____

_____

_____

This is the message which we have heard from
Him and declare to you, that God is light and in
Him is no darkness at all.
I John 1:5 (NKJV)

Scripture tells us that God is light, but what is light? Scientifically, light is described as electromagnetic radiation; a force of energy visible to the human eye. It is said to be an agent that makes things visible by stimulating sight. This indicates that man can control light, but this light that man turns off and on is only artificial.

John spoke about a Light that pierces all darkness. Our Lord does not make light, or provide light, our God IS Light. The Light that drives out darkness and reveals the flaws and impurities of His people. John writes that "God is light and in Him is no darkness at all (I John 1:5)."

God is holy, man is not; but men may join in the pure light of the Lord and walk in His fellowship when they choose to illuminate His light within their lives. If we allow Him to penetrate the darkness of our sins with His light, we may bask in the pure and perfect light of our Lord.

This is the message which we have heard from
Him and declare to you, that God is light and in
Him is no darkness at all.
I John 1:5 (NKJV)

Dear Father in heaven,

Cover me with Your light so that the darkness of my sins might be expelled and Your radiance might shine through.

_____

_____

_____

_____

_____

_____

_____

_____

_____

_____

_____

_____

If we say we have fellowship with Him, and walk in darkness,
we lie and do not practice the truth. But if we walk in the light,
as He is the light, we have fellowship with one another, and the
blood of Jesus Christ, His Son, cleanses us from all sin.
I John 1:6-7 (ESV)

O ur Father, God, created us to have a relationship with Him. He is so jealous for us that He craves our fellowship like some of us crave chocolate. The desire is deep and persistent. God wants nothing more than to be the center of our lives. We say we want to have a relationship with God as well. We so easily turn to God on Sundays and during "churchy" events. We revel in the warm embrace of God's light and think that all is good.

Then Monday and Tuesday roll around and we find ourselves stepping outside of that circle of light and into the shadows. Maybe not into the deep corners of the darkness, but certainly beyond the brilliance of God's light. We drop the hand of our God, and take up casual relationship with Darkness. Maybe a disagreement with a spouse or child caused bitter words. Or in the busyness of getting on with life, a neighbor's need is missed. Could it be that there just wasn't time for Scripture and prayer. After all, that is scheduled in on Sunday.

Our heavenly Daddy is waiting with the light on. He desires us all to turn back to Him. He begs us to search out His light and come back to that rightness with Him within his warm circle of light, obscured by sin and selfishness. We can step back into the circle. We can once again know that all is good and renew that fellowship. Repentance and turning away from the darkness allows us to enter that realm of God's perfect Light and once again let Him wrap us up in His love.

> If we say we have fellowship with Him, and walk in darkness,
> we lie and do not practice the truth. But if we walk in the light,
> as He is the light, we have fellowship with one another, and the
> blood of Jesus Christ, His Son, cleanses us from all sin.
> I John 1:6-7 (ESV)

Sweet Jesus,

I ask You to keep that light burning. I thank You for loving me so much that You desire a relationship with me. Thank You for shedding light on me to illuminate my sin so I will see it and turn away from it. I pray I might squelch the sin and follow Your lighted path back to good fellowship with You. Thank You for lighting my way.

Whoever says, "I am in the light", while hating a brother or sister, is still in the darkness. Whoever loves a brother or sister lives in the light, and in such a person, there is no cause for stumbling.
I John 2:9-10 (RSV)

J ohn goes straight to the point with this Scripture. He makes one squirm when he asserts that we are outside of God's Light when we hate another. But hate can be an ambiguous word. We find ourselves justifying our actions by denying that we hate that annoying coworker or the nasty back door neighbor. We hide behind hate by telling ourselves that only bad people hate. We really dislike that certain someone, but that is not really hate. Anyway the neighbors deserve it because they were the ones who started the argument when they spoke ill of the Christmas decorations on our roof last year.

Christians speak ill of politicians but don't call it hate because the politician is not someone they know personally. Christians speak ill of the criminal that is the hot topic on the evening news, but that is ok because they don't know him either and he is a bad man. Christians speak ill of the folks that sit behind them at Church on Sunday then behave in an unseemly manner through the week, but that is ok because it is righteous judgment.

Some will hold firm that these bad thoughts are not hate unless one takes those feelings and does something about them. Hate isn't really hate until a person acts on that emotion. However, Webster defines hate as "regard with strong aversion or ill will; detest; find unpalatable or unappealing". Nowhere in this definition is there anything stated about "doing" hate. Simply thinking ill about another is hate and that puts us in the darkness. We are outside of the precious light of God when we hate our brother or sister.

Oh but, that politician and that criminal are not my brother or sister. Wrong again! We are all sons and daughters of Christ and therefore, that stranger in the news is our relative through our Father in heaven. Jesus died for the sins of all, giving everyone the same chance to eternal heritage. We can't pick and choose who we wish to hate and who we wish to love. John reminds us that we are not to hate anyone. Rather, if we want to walk in the light of Christ we are commanded to love our brother and sister.

Our society has dimmed that spiritual Light allowing us to believe that hate is ok as long as we do not hurt someone. That hate, however, turns our eyes and heart from God and toward the darkness. He tells us that "whoever loves his brother and sister walks in the light and does not stumble". Let's turn away from the diluted message of our contemporary culture and move purposefully towards God's bright Light to show the world how Christian love really shines.

Whoever says, "I am in the light", while hating a brother or sister,
is still in the darkness. Whoever loves a brother or sister lives in the light,
and in such a person, there is no cause for stumbling.
I John 2:9-10 (RSV)

Lord God,

Convict me of the sin of hate. Open my eyes so that I might see through the darkness of the popular notion that it is ok to hate some folks. Remind me yet again that all are Your people and set my sights so that I see those who annoy me or I find unappealing through a lens of Christian love. I so want to be in Your light Father. Take my hand and lead the way.

_____

_____

_____

_____

_____

_____

_____

_____

_____

_____

After this I saw another angel coming down from heaven,
having great authority;
and the earth was made bright with his splendor.
Rev. 18:1 (NRSV)

"The earth was made bright with His splendor." Can you just imagine? Can you feel the excitement? Can you feel the power? Are you trembling with fear and anticipation?

In trying to wrap my brain around what this brightness might be like, I am reminded of a time when I was in the emergency room following a cat bite that required emergency surgery on my hand. It was broad daylight and the lights were on in the surgery room, but when the doctor began the procedure on my hand, he directed a bright beam right on the center of the wound. Everything in the room paled against this direct and intentional placement of the light. Another time I remember being center stage at a dance recital. As the heavy curtain slowly drew back, the spot light beamed down on the dancers and was blinding and almost painful in its intensity.

Even so, this Light that will come down from heaven, covering all of the earth in its brightness, will be so very intense that nothing we have experienced before will come close to that radiant glory of our God. I believe we will fall to our knees wide-eyed with fear and reverence as we bask in the radiance of that beam. Our Lord and Savior will cover every inch of this earth with His blinding Light to remind us yet again that He is sovereign and will reign forever. His brightness makes everything else in this life pale under its beam. Our Lord will shine His Light to expose the evil and the righteous alike, and the intensity could be blinding and painful.

Dear friend, Scripture tells us that authority is coming. Let's be ready to accept the brightness with our faces up and our hearts full of anticipation for the splendor of our King.

"After this I saw another angel coming down from heaven,
having great authority;
and the earth was made bright with his splendor."
Rev. 18:1 (NRSV)

Sweet Jesus,

I ask that You illuminate our hearts and lives on this earth in a way that makes us bright with Your splendor. I pray that we might be ready for Your arrival and anxiously anticipate the moment we will be bathed in Your penetrating Light.

_____

_____

_____

_____

_____

_____

_____

_____

_____

_____

_____

The city has no need of the sun or the moon to shine on it,
because the glory of God shines on it, and the Lamb is its lamp.
Revelation 21:23 (GNT)

The New Jerusalem is described in the book of Revelation in such a way that I cannot even fathom how beautiful it will be. John tells us that it will have twelve foundations and will be bigger than anything we can imagine. The city will be of pure gold and every kind of jewel will adorn its walls. But the sun, nor the moon, will be present because the King of Kings will give it all the Light it needs. God's glory will illuminate the new city.

Oh how I wish that God's glory illuminated my city today. We so need to be filled with that warmth and splendor. If we allowed God to light the corners of our homes, our petty issues would be resolved. If we allowed God to light the corners of our places of employment, we would enjoy our eight-hour work day so much more. If we allowed

God to light the corners of our churches, we could be such great servants to those in need.

When God's glory shines on us we could be as brilliant as those jewels in the New Jerusalem. We could spread His penetrating Light in amazing ways in our homes, our jobs, and our churches. Why are we afraid to do that? God promises us that if we are about His work, He will give us the tools that we need to get the job done. Let's start radiating God's Light today!

The city has no need of the sun or the moon to shine on it,
because the glory of God shines on it, and the Lamb is its lamp.
Revelation 21:23 (GNT)

Oh Father,

How I long to see that city on which Your glory shines. How I long to be in that place that is so filled with You that it needs no sun or moon to light it. Father, help me to make my little place on this earth as bright as I can make it until that day that I join You in eternity.

_____

_____

_____

_____

_____

_____

_____

_____

_____

_____

_____

_____

The grace of our Lord Jesus Christ be with you all. Amen.
Revelation 22:21 (NKJV)

G race is generally defined as God's unmerited favor. It is the word "unmerited" that trips us up. We find ourselves in a world that demands multi-tasking on a day-to-day basis. We labor for power, wealth, status, happiness, and success only to find that our desires are really never sated.

True satisfaction will only be found when we submit ourselves to the grace (that unmerited favor) of our Lord Jesus Christ. Because He is the Light, His favor is permeated with light and is able to shine in the most remote recesses of our hearts, our minds and our lives. His grace is always sufficient!

Did you notice God's Word doesn't end with the words "The End". We are told that Jesus is the Alpha and the Omega, beginning and the end. God said, "Let there be light," and there was. He commanded the guiding light to the Babe, who was born in a manger, and His Guiding Light still leads us. We are promised a New Jerusalem which will require neither the sun nor the moon, but will be exuberantly lit by God's Holy Light. Amen.

The grace of our Lord Jesus Christ be with you all. Amen.
Revelation 22:21 (NKJV)

Thank You Jesus for being our Guiding Light and giving us the Holy Spirit who enables us to share Your light with the world. May the world see a glimmer of Your grace through our lives, and to God be the Glory.

_____

_____

_____

_____

_____

_____

_____

_____

_____

CPSIA information can be obtained at www.ICGtesting.com
Printed in the USA
LVOW120703010513

331729LV00001B/1/P

9 781936 746392